UNLOCK YOUR FIRE TV STICK LIKE A PRO

& Install KODI in 15 Min. or Less

Table of Contents

GENERAL MAINTENANCE

To keep your connections and streaming running smooth and trouble free from any buffering issues, then you need to perform general maintenance of your Network- and we recommend to do this weekly. To start, unplug your Fire TV Device, unplug your Modem and Router to reset your Network. Leave them unplugged for 1 minute minimum. Then first plug in your Modem and let it fully boot and connect to your Internet Service (up to 5 min. sometimes). Next plug in your Wireless Wifi Router to power and give it time to make a connection. Lastly plug in your Fire TV Device.

We recommend doing this before starting any of the installation procedures we are going to cover below in this Tutorial!
90% of issues can be fixed by un-plugging your Fire TV Device and allowing it to Reset! Try this FIRST FOR ANY Buffering or Connectivity issues!

**This user guide is for Educational Purposes only & we assume absolutely NO responsibility for your actions or how you decide to use it.

Installing Kodi

Hello and welcome to our interactive Tutorial where you will learn step by step how the pros have been installing KODI successfully for many many years with great results. We realize there is a lot of mis-guided information out there on the internet these days and have made it our ultimate goal to get you informed on a proper install that simply just works! Believe us when we tell you, we have tried EVERYTHING under the sun! Some Kodi builds will work for just a short while then fail, and leave you stranded wondering what to do. Feel free to visit (www.firesticksource.com) our site is full of useful information and you will have the added benefit of reaching out to our Support Team to ask any questions you may have through any of your install process. Support guarantees a reply within 24 hrs, but on most cases will get back to you much quicker then that. If you need assistance, please contact us through our "Support" tab on our website. You will find it in lower lefthand corner of webpage. On Mobile it is displayed as a "?"

So, first let's talk about what Exactly Kodi is. Kodi is the ultimate entertainment center software. It plays almost every kind of media you can find and it looks great while doing it! It's important to remember, Kodi is just a "Blank Platform" media player. Many people confuse this and think that Kodi itself provides all of the content we are seeking, but that is not the case at all. All of your Free Content (Movies, Live TV etc.) are provided through 3rd party Add ons that we will install inside of Kodi. We have taken the top 100 Add ons and compiled them into one place. This is called a "Build" and you've probably heard the term before if you've done any type of research on a "Kodi Box". Many sellers out there just take low quality (sometimes outdated) free builds they scrounged up and install them in Kodi and sell them to the end consumer. Problem with this is, the build may work at first, but the Add ons will eventually become outdated sometimes within a week or two, and the unit will begin to fail and always provide dead links. This leaves the end consumer with a poor experience. Our build that we are providing is backed by a great group of guys that are constantly developing and pushing new updates and features and that's what sets the MisFit Mods Group apart from the rest! With these updates your unit will always stay fresh and working, as even tiny updates and tweaks to the builds are made even daily. This is why it is important to always stay updated.

Getting Started

To start you will need either an
Amazon Fire TV Stick or Amazon Fire TV Box

If you don't already have one feel free to visit Amazon so you can get one Ordered. This Tutorial applies to all of the streaming units Amazon offers. Fire TV Box will be much more Responsive than Stick

Fire TV Stick

All-New Fire TV

	Fire TV Stick	All-New Fire TV
Price	$39.99	$69.99
Supported resolution	Up to 1080p HD at 60 fps	Up to 4K Ultra HD at 60 fps
HDR-10 support		✓
Alexa Voice Remote	✓	✓
Hands-free voice control with any Echo device	✓	✓
Quad-core processor	1.3 GHz	1.5 GHz
Memory	1 GB	2 GB
Storage	8 GB	8 GB
Supported audio	Dolby Audio	Dolby Atmos
802.11ac dual-band MIMO Wi-Fi	✓	✓
Compatible with Amazon Ethernet Adapter	✓	✓

Getting Started

(Brand New Device)

For those of you who just ordered a Brand New Fire TV Device follow the instructions below to setup your Device:

1. Open the Box- you'll need the contents of the box, a Wifi connection (recommended high speed internet), a Wifi password if required, and a TV with a HDMI Port.
2. Plug in your Fire TV Stick- Insert the Fire TV Stick into one of the HDMI Ports on your TV, use the HDMI Extender cord as it will Help boost your WIFI Signal to your device! Connect the power adapter to the Fire TV Stick, and plug it into a wall outlet. Turn on your TV, and select the applicable HDMI input source.
3. Follow the on-screen guide- An on-screen guide will help you setup your Fire TV Stick. You will probably need to connect your remote to your Fire Stick, follow on screen instructions. If remote won't connect, try holding Home Button for 10+ seconds-then release.
4. Registration- Either register the Fire TV Stick to your current Amazon account or create a new account. (Both are Free) It's best to register New Accounts on a Computer, then login to the device on your T.V.

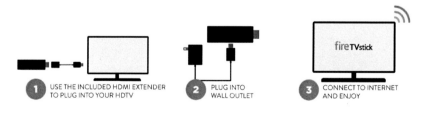

For best results, use the included HDMI extender for improved Wi-Fi connectivity.

Getting Started

(Already own a Device)

It's always best practice to just start with a fresh clean slate to install on, so if you are going to be installing Kodi and other apps onto this device let's go ahead and perform a factory reset. Don't worry, as any Apps you've previously purchased from Amazon will remain in your cloud and will be automatically synced after you login.

To Start:
From "HOME"> Scroll Right & Click into "Settings"
Scroll Right again & Click into "Device"
at the bottom of the Menu> Select "Reset to Factory Defaults">"Reset"
It will take some where around 10 minutes for the Device to Reset to Factory Default Settings.
Once device is finished and ready, go ahead and login, setup Wifi network and go through initial setup until you reach the main Amazon home screen.
Check for Updates:
From "HOME"> Scroll Right & Click into "Settings"
Scroll Right again & Click into "Device" > About > Check for System Update (If available, download & install)

Amazon Home Screen

Now that we have a fresh slate to install Kodi on, *Starting from Amazon Home Screen scroll right to "Settings"> Device > Developer Options & Turn On both "ADB Debugging" & "Apps from Unknown Sources"* now hit the Home 🏠 Button once more. With those options now enabled we can begin by using the search function 🔍 just to the left of "Home" Type in "Downloder"

Select and go ahead and install Downloader for Free.

TIP: You might need to Enable 1-Click settings within your Amazon account to be able to install Apps. Visit http://amazon.com/mykps to setup 1-Click on a web browser...

After installation, open the Downloader App. Now type in the following URL. Make sure it matches EXACTLY
https://kodi.tv/download
Then click "Go"

Scroll down and select Android

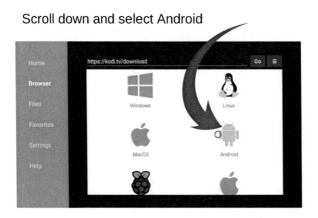

Now you want to choose "ARMV7A (32BIT)
It's the upper middle blue box choice

Let Kodi download and click "Install"... once prompted click "Open"
Kodi will prepare for it's 1st run, and then open to the Empty Default screen
you see pictured below... (Menu may differ slightly in future KODI Updates)

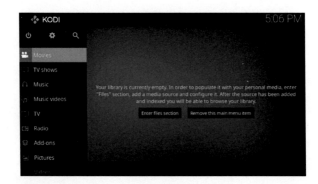

Open "Settings" by clicking the small gear at top center of menu

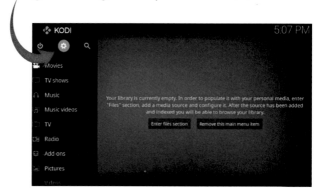

Now go ahead and choose "System Settings"

Scroll down to "Add-Ons" then over to "Unknown Sources"
We want to make sure and Enable this setting

Press the back button on your remote, and click into "File Manager"

Add Source

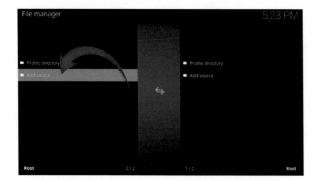

Click into "<None>"

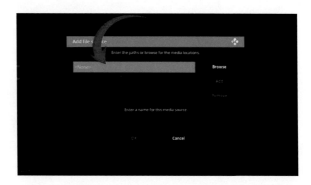

Type in the following URL EXACTLY how it shows:
http://misfitmods.com/mmwiz/repo
Then go ahead and click "OK"

Scroll down and choose "OK" once more, press the back button on your remote twice until you are at Main Kodi Menu again where we initially started. Scroll down and click "Add-ons"

Click small open box icon in upper left corner

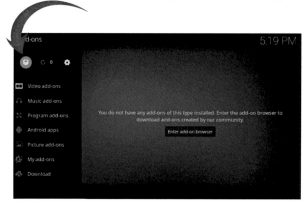

Scroll down and click on "Install from zip file"

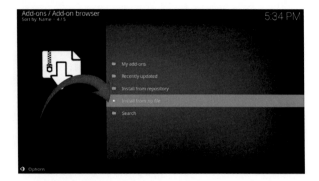

Choose "repo" from the choices

Now choose "repository.misfitmods.zip"

Wait about 5 seconds and you will receive a notification Pop-up after it installs...now scroll up one option and click into "Install from repository"

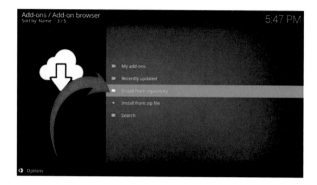

Now click into "misfit mods: Repository"

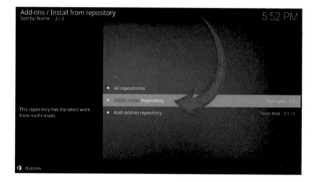

Choose> "Program add-ons"> then "Misfit Mods Wizard"
Now you want to go ahead and "Install"

You will see a notification that the Misfit Mods Wizard Add-on has successfully been installed...

Now choose> "Dismiss"> "Continue"> and choose "Build Menu"
This will take you into the MisFit Mods Builds Menu. We will be choosing to install the Famous & Best Build available named "HardNox".

You can choose Link 1 or Link 2 both are the same file. Link 2 usually has less traffic and will download faster. Mornings are better than nights (less traffic) ***Note-after updates are pushed this screen might look a little different but you always want to choose HardNox if you want reliability and Great options!*

It's worth noting here, that with the Build Menu, you could essentially pick from any builds on the list if you really wanted to. For Example "BLITZ" build is a "Sports ONLY" build and some might enjoy that. Or you have "Kids Room" which has only content suitable for Kids. "Desire" is a female driven build, "Misfit Mods Lite" is a great build to install on the Older 1st Gen Fire Sticks as it is very minimal, and that Fire Stick only has half the processing power as the Newer Gen 2 w/ Alexa Remote does. So it would run much smoother when not packed full of Add-ons. Anyway, we will go over how to perform updates later on and you could always experiment and check out the other builds then. For now... We highly suggest "HardNox" Build because of its Successful History and we've installed this build on Literally THOUSANDS of Fire Sticks and boxes in the past! It gets constant Updates and has literally anything you could ever want from 3rd party Add-ons inside of Kodi! All of these Builds are subject to change and might or might not be available when you read this. We strive to always improve and exceed the last version of everything we put out, so it only gets better :)

Back to our install now....

When you click on 1 of the 2 Install Links you will be asked if you want to perform a Fresh Install or a Standard Install. For an initial install of our Build inside of Kodi, we will choose *"Standard Install" > then "Yes Install"*

Depending on the Amount of people currently downloading from the Servers and your internet speed, it can take anywhere from 2 minutes to 30 min.

Let the Files download to your Device and Fully Extract...be patient and do not hit Cancel. If for some reason you get multiple errors or you have to start over, make sure you choose *"Fresh Install"* so that the Wizard can clean out all of the previous Files to start a Fresh Download.

Once files are extracted you will want to choose *"Force Close"*

Now it will exit you into the "Downloader App" just exit out of there by clicking the back button & then press the Home button on your remote

Congratulations! You have Successfully installed our Custom Misfit Mods Kodi Build on your Device. After you let it sit for about 20 seconds, go ahead and open up the Kodi App.

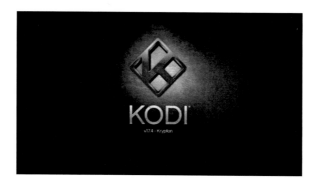

It's VERY important that each time you open Kodi, you let it sit there for atleast 3-5 minutes before navigating, so that it can load up the Menu, Force Add-on updates, Clear Cache etc. Doing so, will allow a much smoother Experience.

After updates are finished, you are free to use the Program as you wish. Watch Free Movies, stream live T.V. etc. The HardNox build is packed with Add-ons and there are multiple ways to access the content you are seeking, so just take your time to learn your way around.

About Kodi

• Navigate through Main Menu by scrolling Left or Right. Once an option is selected either click into it, or click down to the Sub-Menu below it to find what you are seeking.

•If you click up above the Main Menu, you will enter the Widgets set for that specific Menu item

• To Quit Kodi and have it restart for you, scroll to *"SYSTEM"* > *"QUIT"* from sub menu below. If you just hit your home button on your remote- Kodi is left running in Background. Most issues can be fixed by a "Force Stop" by allowing a Fresh Startup. If for some reason any of the Apps freeze or won't load, you can go to the Main Amazon Home Page. *Click into "Settings" > "Applications" > "Manage Installed Applications" > then "KODI" & finally "Force Stop"* or just unplug your Device for 30 Seconds…

• Search for Streams that work for you. It is important to understand Kodi is an Open Source program and we rely on 3rd Party Developers to Deliver us this "FREE CONTENT". To learn your way around, you will just have to take some time to Explore and Familiarize yourself with the Program. Remember, not everything works that's just the way it is and its been like that since Kodi came out. We rely on 3rd party Developers to keep their services up to date and Servers online. Sometimes Links will be down or crowded, other times they will work. If a Developer of an Add-on steps down, they usually pass their work onto another so the service can be brought back to Life (sometimes under a new Add-on Name)

• The HardNox Build incorporates the Top 100 working Kodi Add ons, so you will Always have the BEST of the BEST!

• The best spot for Movies, Shows etc at this time is Covenant (New-Exodus). You can find that under the Sub Menu of "Movies". For "TV Shows" Exodus is the #1 Top Pick for most of the Kodi Community for a while now. Definetly take the time to explore and learn which Add on you like the best!

• At this time, Exodus is great for Searching through Networks and finding your Exact Network, Shows, and Specific Seasons for Viewing but that could always change in the future.

• Understanding how it all works: When you pick content on Kodi to Stream to your Fire TV device, you are in essence forwarding your request to Providers (Servers) who are hosting this content. Kodi loads all of the available options into a list of Links for you to choose from. Kodi then displays that list to you, and you can choose which Link you would like to Stream the content from. Most of the Higher Quality Links (HD/1080p) will be located towards top of your options (usually 1st or 2nd etc)

• In Theaters Movies- When Movies just barely come out in Movie Theaters they may show up on Kodi within a day or two or before. With our Experience the Quality will be very pour, or even a Camera Rip from the theater. Just give it a few days to a week and there usually will be a HD or higher quality Link posted. Just be patient!

• Follow the News about Kodi, so you can keep yourself updated!!

• Cut the Cable & Enjoy Free Entertainment!

Adult Content

Adult content- Each time you install our MisFit Mods HardNox build, it will be loaded with Adult Content, but it is hidden from the Main Menu. If you would like to Enable it Follow these Instructions below! (you can disable it again- anytime)

• *Scroll on the Kodi Main Menu and click into "System" > "Interface" > "Skin" > "Configure Skin" > "Setup the Aeon Nox Main Menu"*

• *Click to the Left Side and Scroll down the Menu Titles and Highlight "AFTER DARK" > Long Press the Center Select Button on the Remote > then Enable.* This will Add the XXX to the Main Menu.

• Click back arrow all the way out to Main Menu Screen and give it a minute to Update the Skin and you are all set.

• To Disable the XXX again and Ultimately hide it on Main Menu Follow instructions above the same, just click *"Disable"*

Updating Kodi

It is OKAY & Important to UPDATE your Custom Build inside KODI when new updates are Released! Whenever you are Prompted to Update your - Kodi Build-or Experiencing any Errors etc-Always do it! Usually you will receive a Pop-Up notifying you of a new Update Available, but to manually update your MisFits Mods build inside Kodi, follow these instructions.

Start by navigating left or right in the Main Menu of Kodi until you find "Programs" click down below into the Sub menu and click into "Builds Menu". If you cannot locate this it can also be found under "Mis Fit Mods Wizard"

This should look familiar to you, as its the same Build Menu as before when we did the initial install. All you are going to do is choose the HardNox link (again, Link 1 & Link 2 are the exact same) if one doesn't work, then use the other.

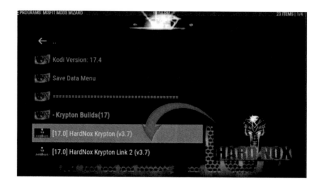

You MUST choose "FRESH INSTALL" otherwise the new updated Build will conflict with the older version. Fresh Install will remove all the old files, and install everything within Kodi fresh and new for you. Once downloaded and extracted you will want to choose "Force Close" just like last time.

This is how you can change builds as well if you have the inclination to do so... just remember that HardNox is tried and true!
Like we said before, we are constantly tweaking with the build and trying to improve upon it any way we can, so as to provide a Premium Smooth Experience for everyone.

After you install the Build inside of Kodi, it is VERY IMPORTANT THAT YOU DO NOT RESTORE, CLEAR DATA OR INSTALL A FRESH START IN KODI. You can restart it, unplug it to move it, change the WIFI source, but DO NOT RESET TO FACTORY DEFAULTS or you will wipe your device and have to start all over from the beginning.

Installing Mobdro

In this section we will go over how you can install Mobdro to your device and stream live television whenever you want for free. Let's start by explaining just what Mobdro is, and how it works first. Mobdro is a tool that constantly looks for free video streams available on the web and makes them accessible on your device. Mobdro has two versions: Freemium and Premium. Freemium is completely free, the Premium version has extras features, like capturing streams and ChromeCast support, and is free of ads. We have had great results just using the Free version for many years now, and Mobdro is very reliable. Every once in a while you will click on a specific channel or network and it will be down, when this happens Mobdro automatically kicks into a search mode, and is searching the web for an available resource to get that channel back online. So, just check back soon, and it will be up and playing again before you know it.

To begin, we will need to first download an App named "ES Explorer" from the Amazon search function. Push your Home 🏠 Button on your remote and then scroll left to Search 🔍 go ahead and type in "Es Explorer" and select it.

You will be taken to the next screen, where you will click on and Download "Es File Explorer" to your device.

It will begin to install...

Press the back button on remote if you receive a pop up ad. then go ahead and click on "Favorite" on the left side of the menu screen

Now click "Add"

Click into "Path" and you want to type the following URL EXACTLY like this: **https://www.mobdro.to/mobdro.apk**   then click "Next"... go ahead and add a Name as well. We will name it "Mobdro". Now click "Add"

Now scroll down on left side and click on the Favorite we just created, it will be named "Mobdro"

This will open the web browser in the window, you now need to locate the 3 dots in lower right corner named "More" and click them, then choose "Open in Browser"

Choose the option "ES Downloader". After download completes choose to "Open File" and then Click "Install" and finally "Install" again...

Once it finishes installing choose "Done", now navigate to the upper left side of ES Explorer and click into "Settings"

Now scroll down and click into "Logger floating widget settings"

You want to Disable/ uncheck the Floating Widget and that will remove the annoying little blue circle you see on your screen :)

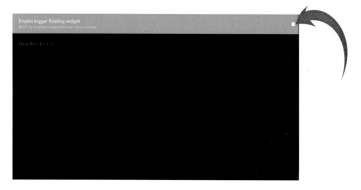

Press your back button twice on your remote, and then press the Home 🏠 button. Scroll down and find the Mobdro App. Congratulations you've successfully installed Mobdro!

Inside of Mobdro, you will find their brand new beautiful interface where you can Explore Channels, News, Shows, Movies, Sports, Music, Gaming, Animals, Tech, Podcasts, Spiritual as well as LIVE content!

Mobdro is loaded with Live TV channels, you can take advantage of the Parental Filter if needed and it will block any channels that might display Adult content. You can sort all of your Favorite Channels in the order you would like them displayed in the menu. Anytime that you are prompted about a New Update, always choose to install it and Mobdro will continue to run Flawlessly on your Device. Enjoy!

Installing Gears TV

Welcome into the next section of our Tutorial where we will walk you step by step through installing Gears TV on your Fire TV Device. Gears TV is considered a Premium IPTV Service. Meaning that there is a monthly subscription fee to have an account setup so that you can Login and use the Service. Gears TV is currently at the TOP of the Game when it comes to Paid Premium IPTV Live Streaming in 1080P & HD! We can guarantee a 95% non buffer, and Super Crystal Clear playback when using this Service. It has been industry tested and Exceeds our Expectations when it comes to a Reliable User Experience.

If you are looking for a Super Low Cost, High Efficiency, Premium and Reliable alternative to Cable or Dish, the Gears TV Platform is the Service for you. When you pair Gears TV Subscription and our Custom Kodi Build on a Fire TV device, you can take advantage of the Fully Functional Interactive TV Guide which will give a True Cable TV Experience without Breaking your Wallet. With the Gears TV Subscription you will get the majority of the Premium Channels, HBO, Showtime, Cinemax, and Starz that most Cable companies offer, along with all of the basic Channels such as TNT, USA, TBS, and much more all in 1080P or HD! Over 300+ Channels!

This is why we are offering the service without any contracts or that BS the Cable and Dish providers hit you with. It's Affordable, it's reliable and it just really works great. To learn how to Sign up to activate your Gears TV App please visit our website at:
https://www.firesticksource.com/gears-tv

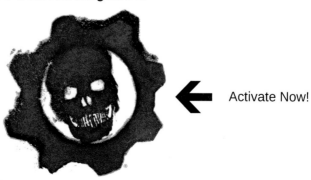

Activate Now!

Getting Started

In order to install the Gears TV App on your device, we will be using the "ES File Explorer" App that we used in the previous Chapter when we downloaded Mobdro. Both processes are very similar, but we will still break down the steps needed for you.

To begin, you will want to Launch the "ES File Explorer" App from the Main Amazon Home page...

Press the back button on remote if you receive a pop up ad. then go ahead and click on "Favorite" on the left side of the screen menu

Now click "Add"

Click into "Path" and you want to type the following URL EXACTLY like this: **http://targetcreates.com/apk**   then click "Next"... go ahead and add a Name as well. We will name it "Gears TV". Now click "Add"

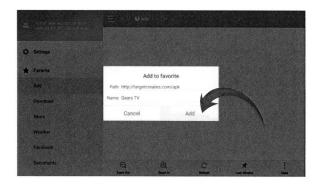

Now scroll down on left side and click on the Favorite we just created it will be named "Gears TV"

Now you want to click to the right and highlight and click the 2nd File it will be named "GearsTV_Master-release-arm.apk"

Now we need to locate the 3 dots in lower right corner named "More" and click them, then choose "Open in Browser"

Choose the option "ES Downloader". After download completes choose to "Open File" and then Click "Install" and finally "Install" again...

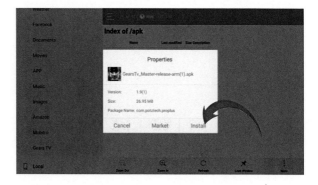

Once it finishes installing choose "Done"... this will drop you back into Es File Explorer, go ahead and just click the Home 🏠 Button on your remote to take you back to the Main Amazon Home Screen.
Congratulations, you have successfully installed Gears TV App on your Fire TV device.
Don't forget to visit:
www.firesticksource.com/gears-tv to get Activated!

Login screen for Gears TV. Each time you launch Gears TV App it will automatically check for any new updates...

Using Gears TV
Inside of Kodi

The MisFit Mods HardNox build has a place under the "PREM IPTV" section that will allow you to login and Experience your Gears TV from within Kodi. You can get there by opening the Kodi app and letting it load. After a few minutes (loading, clearing cache etc.) scroll left or right in the Main Menu bar until you see "PREM IPTV"

**Theres a chance that Not every version HardNox Kodi Build will contain a PREM IPTV Section- if this is the case watch these videos at this link:
www.firesticksource.com/resources

Scroll down into the Sub Menu, and click into the Gears TV Add-on, you will be greeted with this screen.

Make sure you have your Login Credentials ready so we can begin Login

You will need to choose "YES" so that we can enter our Username & Password...

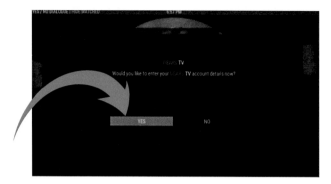

Use your remote to enter your Username then choose "Done"... Now repeat that for your Password. You will be logged in, and should not have to enter your Credentials again unless you update the build etc.

Once logged in you will be taken to this Menu screen...

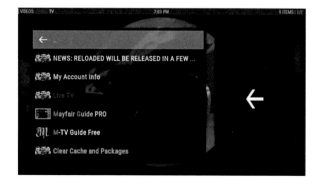

To view any of the Live TV channels, scroll to "Live TV" and click in...

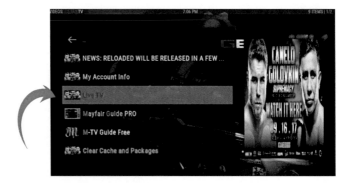

Choose the section you would like to watch...

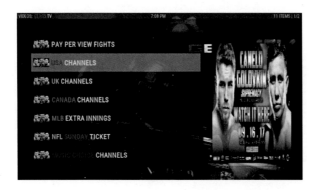

Now you are able to scroll between Channels, and choose what you would enjoy viewing. Press the back button on Remote to exit a channel or to get back to the Menu screen.

Installing Mayfair Guide PRO

(TV Guide)

In the following steps we will walk you through setting up the Mayfair Guide Pro to combine with your Gears TV subscription. Mayfair Guide Pro is a complete interactive TV Guide. It will allow you to see what shows are playing, click up/down on your remote to switch between channels, set reminders etc. You are able to customize the Skin and Background image in the TV Guide if you'd like. In our opinion, it really allows you to take full advantage of Gears TV's full potential.

*Note- the M-TV Guide Free is no longer supported with Gears-TV!

Let's start by clicking on "Mayfair Guide PRO" in the main menu

If you get this Pop-up, don't worry, we will show you how to install the Repository so it will work for you

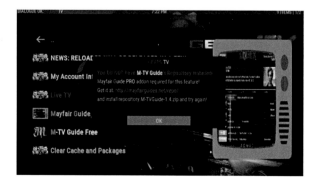

Go ahead and press the back button until you exit Gears TV and are taken to the Main HardNox Kodi menu. Scroll right or left unitl you see "SYSTEM". From the Sub-menu below click "File Manager"

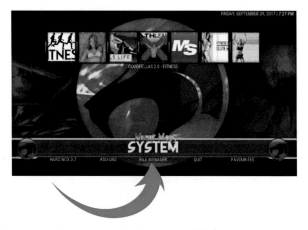

Scroll all the way to bottom and choose "Add Source"

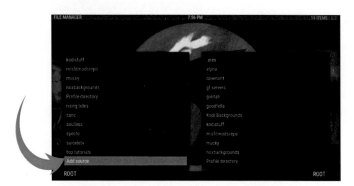

Click on "<None>" and type this URL EXACTLY into the toolbar: **http://mayfairguides.net/repo** then select "Done"

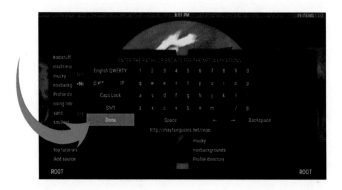

Let's go ahead and Enter our own name for the Media Source. Clear out "repo" and type in "Mayfair Guide" select "Done" then Click "OK"

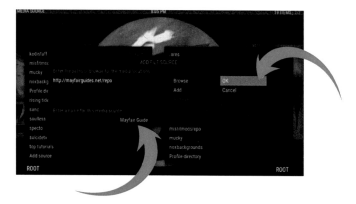

Press back button on remote to take you to the Main HardNox Menu, now under "SYSTEM" you need to click "ADD-ONS"

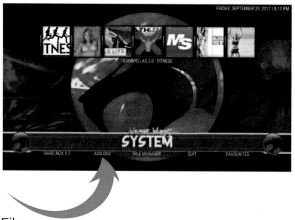

Choose Install from Zip File...

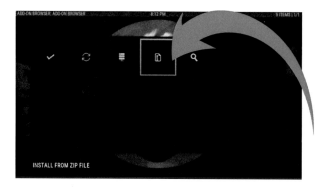

Scroll down and Click on "Mayfair Guide" or whatever you chose to name it from a few steps before...

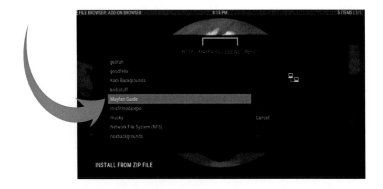

Now click on "repository.M-TVGuide-1.4.zip"

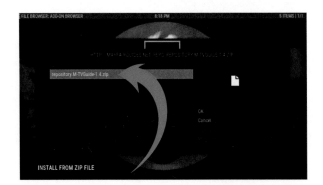

Wait up to 10 seconds... you will see a Pop-up stating that the Add-on was installed....

Now click into "Install from Repository"...

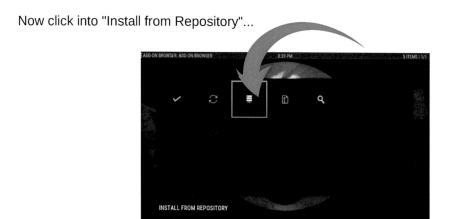

Scroll down and click on "M-TV Guide Repository"...

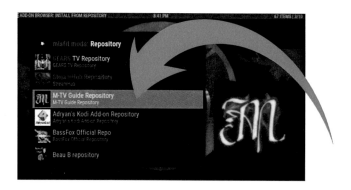

Choose "Program add-ons"...

Select "Mayfair Guide PRO"... and then "Install". If done correctly should say "Enabled"

Now, we want to Navigate back to the Gears TV Add-on inside of Kodi under the "PREM IPTV" section. Once inside click on "Mayfair Guide PRO" once again. You will now be prompted to enter a Username & Password, as this is a paid monthly Subscription. Don't worry, as it is literally DIRT CHEAP! Only around $2.50 a month...
Follow the Instructions in the next Section to setup an account

Subscribing to
Mayfair Guide PRO

1. Go to http://mayfairguides.com/pro/ and click "SUBSCRIBE" at the top of the website or go to https://mayfairguides.com/pro/subscribe
2. Create your account by filling out your details in the form. Remember the Username and Password you create here will be used for both the website and addon login.
3. Click "Add Billing Method" and enter your details and then click "Add"
4. Click "Submit Form" at the bottom right under "Checkout Now" to complete the signup/subscribe process.
Your account is activated automatically after this process was successful.

TIP: Join the "Mayfair Guides" group on Facebook for Support and help for any issues you might encounter. The guys are really good about getting you taken care of!

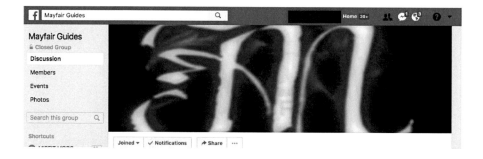

Now let's Login to the Mayfair Guide PRO and select "Done" after you are finished

All of the Necessary files will now begin to Download and install...

You might be greeted with a Pop-up about configuring some settings inside of your Kodi Video Settings. Definetly choose "YES" as it will correct anything that we might have missed...

You should receive a confirmation that your Kodi video settings have been correctly configured.

We have to re-launch Mayfair Guide PRO now, in order for it to work correctly. Press your back button to exit out of Gears TV Add-on, then go right back in. Now launch "Mayfair Guide PRO" from the menu!

Installing and Updating...

SUCCESS! We are ready to Rock and Roll now!

Hold down the "Select/OK" (center button) on your remote and it will bring up the Settings at the top of the TV Guide. You need to take the time to explore the options here. You can customize the Skin in the background, set reminders, organize channels, search channels, set favorites, and perform any maintenance you might need to do in the future...

Exiting Kodi
the Proper Way

It is very important that you exit Kodi the proper way. Doing so, allows Kodi to start up Fresh the next time around, and perform all of the necessary updates for Add-ons, clear the Cache, packages etc. This will allow for a Smoother Experience, and cut back on any errors as well. If you just press the Home 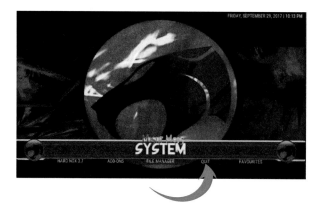 Button on your remote, Kodi is left running in the background... you DO NOT want to do this!

To properly close Kodi out, Navigate the Main Menu from within the HardNox Kodi build to "SYSTEM" click down below into the Sub menu on "QUIT"

Next, you want to choose "FORCE CLOSE KODI" and this will properly shut down the program and keep it from running in the Background.

Trouble Shooting
Kodi

Why am I seeing Errors pop up while i'm in Kodi?

Just because there is an error shown for an Add-on while you are inside of Kodi, does not mean your Kodi Build is non functional. You have to realize, we have near 100 Add-ons loaded inside of this HardNox Build. This is what makes up our Custom Build (the Apps we choose, and Setup for you). Each single Add-on was developed by a different individual then the next. If you see an error, it usually just means that specific Add on failed to communicate with it's home Server, or that an update might be required for better Add-on performance. Our Kodi build Forces Updates upon start up, whether the updates are available or not, is up to the Specific Add-On Developers and completely out of our Hands. Seeing an error, does not specifically mean that Add-on won't work, you can still try it, but if you have issues you will just have to use another until that specific Add-on is updated. Best Practice is to go to "System" then "Quit" in the Sub menu below and "Force Close" Kodi on every exit. This will guarantee a Fresh Start up next time you open it, and Updates will be Forced and Cache & Packages Cleaned for better performance. Also, make sure you are giving Kodi a minimum of 3 minutes to Load all Add-ons, let them call back to home Servers for updates, etc. This will allow for a much smoother experience if you just be patient and give it time.

How do I navigate through Kodi?

Navigate through the Main Menu by scrolling Left or Right. Once an option is selected either click into it, or click down to the Sub-Menu below it to find what you are seeking. **MOST PEOPLE MISS ALL OF THE GOOD ADD ONS LOCATED IN THE SUB MENU!**

Kodi App is Frozen up or Laggy- not working

Try Restarting your Device to fix the Issue. To Restart your Fire TV device, hold down both the "OK/SELECT" center button AND your "PLAY/PAUSE" button on your Remote at the same time for 5 Seconds. Or you can *Navigate to Amazon Home Page>Settings>Device>Restart Device*

Restarting the Device normally fixes 90% of Issues you may be encountering.

Still having an issue? *Navigate to Amazon Home Page>Settings>Applications>Manage Installed Applications> then select the App you are Trouble shooting> Press "Force Stop"*

WARNING NEVER PRESS CLEAR DATA ON KODI APP! YOU WILL ERASE YOUR MisFit Mods BUILD!!! It is okay to "Clear Data" on Gears TV, Mobdro, and IPVanish, just NOT KODI!!

How do I update my Kodi Build?
**NOTE: It is OKAY & Important to UPDATE your Custom Build inside KODI when new updates are Released! Whenever you are Prompted to Update your -Kodi Build-or Experiencing any Errors etc-Always do it! Usually you will Receive a Pop-Up notifying you of a new Update Available, but to Manually Update your MisFits Mods Build inside Kodi: *Open up Kodi App, scroll to "PROGRAMS" in Main Menu click down into the Sub Menu below on "Builds Menu" scroll down to "[17.0] HardNox Krypton (version #)" update to the Newest Version of Hard Nox.* Right now the Newest Update Available is the Top White Link & Choose (Fresh Install) then "Continue". Wait until the New Update is Completely installed then choose "Force Close".
If you cannot locate this it can also be found under "Mis Fit Mods Wizard"

Sometimes (even daily) we push small updates to fix issues, and are always working towards improving Performance, so it never hurts to update your same version once you have the Newest Release. Note* on small little tweaks of the Build like this, the version # of the Build will not change... Stay Fresh :) Updating Weekly won't hurt a thing!

Installing IPVanish
VPN

In this section, we will go over how to install the IPVanish App onto your Fire TV device. This use to be a difficult process to setup and configure the App for use with the Fire TV devices, but IPVanish has since updated the APK and made it available in the Amazon App Store and is pre configured for you! Learn more about why you should be using a VPN for your privacy, on our website at: **www.firesticksource.com/vpn**

Start by pressing the Home ⬠ Button on your remote. Scroll left and click into Search ⃝ type in "Ipvanish" then click on the result.

Now open the IPVanish App and "Install" to your Fire TV Device and "Open"

Now you will be greeted with the Login screen.

You will need to setup an Account with IPVanish to obtain your Login information and be able to use the VPN Service. For the Best Discounted prices visit our website at: **www.firesticksource.com/vpn**

Once you finish your Sign up process, login to the App and it will remember your credentials. It's best practice to **NOT** have any Apps running in the background when you "Connect" your VPN!!! Our suggestion is to unplug and restart your device that way you can guarantee all Apps have been stopped. "Connect" your IPVanish VPN very FIrst thing **BEFORE** opening any other App! This will allow each App's internet traffic to be directed through the VPN and keep you safe from any prying eyes! All Traffic will then be 100% Military grade encrypted and tunneled, bypassing your Internet Service Provider! Can help if you are being Throttled back!

TIP: a quick and easy way to Restart your Fire TV Device is to hold down the Play/pause button and the center Select button on your remote for 5 seconds.

Conclusion

Congratulations, you've successfully walked yourself through an entire install of one of the Best Kodi builds out there! You've learned how to use Downloader & ES File Explorer to install from online sources, and hopefully have picked up on some tips and tricks along the way that maybe you hadn't known before. Stay up on your General Maintenance of cycling your Device, Router, and Modem off atleast once a week and always do it before installing a Fresh Build! Learn what works for you, and we really wish you luck in your Cable cutting journey! You now have the knowledge to help out your Friends & Family and save them from being raped by these Satellite and Cable companies!

Made in the USA
San Bernardino, CA
18 January 2018